Mother Nature's Party

Julie Bajda

Copyright © 2023 Julie Bajda
All rights reserved
First Edition

PAGE PUBLISHING
Conneaut Lake, PA

First originally published by Page Publishing 2023

ISBN 979-8-88654-190-8 (pbk)
ISBN 979-8-88654-198-4 (digital)

Printed in the United States of America

This book is dedicated to
My four lovely nieces
and my great niece
For whom this story was written

With special thanks to
The Nature in my garden
Which was a source of inspiration

And to C. Edward Caldwell for his guidance
And Zhen for her encouragement and support

A soft rain had fallen overnight as a *gentle breeze* blew.
Mother Nature had been washing and cleaning the garden while everyone was asleep.

Everything in the garden was fresh and sparkling.
The sun began to rise. It was shining on the drops of rain that were clinging to the flowers and the blades of grass.

The animals woke and bathed. They were all very excited!

They had to get busy gathering food to bring to this afternoon's party in the garden.

While Robin was up bright and early, digging for *fat, juicy worms…*

Sam and Sally Squirrel were busy collecting kernels of corn.

Mother Nature spread out a checkered cloth on the grass where the party would be held.

She had even set out bouquets of flowers in a rainbow of colors to add to the festivities.

The sun was shining on the raindrops, so the flowers looked like they were dressed in diamonds for the special occasion.

Cheerful red carnations welcomed their friends into the garden.

Orange and yellow lilies and blue and purple irises dazzled the guests with their beauty.

As the animals began to arrive, there was excitement in the air!

The friends chirped, squealed, squawked, and chattered as they greeted one another.

A colony of ants marched in. They were carrying cheese and cracker crumbs they had found on the patio of the Big House.

(The Big House sat on the garden property.)

Jay, the Blue Jay, brought crunchy sunflower seeds to eat.

Gordy and Goldie Finch brought tasty tidbits of thistle seeds to the feast. Charlie and Chelsea Chipmunk came. Their cheeks were full of grains, and the Rabbit family brought some delicious carrots, beans, and lettuce.

They found these vegetables in Farmer Greene's field on their way to the party.

Mr. and Mrs. Ruby Hummingbird brought sweet nectar to drink, Mr. and Mrs. Cardinal brought fresh berries for dessert, and the Bees brought honey to share.

There was plenty to eat for everyone!

Just then, Rob the Raccoon came into the garden. He wanted to see what was going on.

"Oh, no!" the animals squealed in a nervous panic. "Who invited Rob to the party? We don't want him here. He's a thief—he'll steal all our food!"

Mother Nature told everyone to calm down.

"Be kind," she said softly. "There's plenty to eat for everyone. If we show Rob that we are willing to share, he won't steal from anyone."

Mother Nature told her guests that all things are a part of nature, even Rob. Since it was her party, she invited him to stay.

Everyone welcomed Rob and shared their feast with him. The party continued.

Entertainment included several tunes by the Wind Chimes as well as a charming Waltz of the Flowers as they danced to classical music played by The Fiddling Crickets.

At the end of the day, as darkness fell over the garden, lightning bugs added the finishing touch!

They lit up the evening sky with flashes of light, creating their own *spectacular fireworks show!*

As all of the animals went home for the night, they were happy and well-fed.

Everyone agreed: it had been a wonderful day!

They couldn't wait to do it again!

About the Author

Julie is a retired elementary school teacher. She taught thirty-five years for North Ridgeville City Schools in Ohio. She retired in 2009 and has been a substitute teacher since that time.

During her career, in the lower elementary grades, Julie instilled a love of nature with her students. She also enjoyed teaching creative writing and got her students involved in the Young Authors Program where they wrote and illustrated their own stories.

Julie also loves to travel. She enjoys meeting new people and learning about new cultures.

She has had the fortunate experience of teaching English summer school to very young children in Stary Sacz and Nowy Sacz in southern Poland.

The use of colorful picture books proved to be a very valuable asset during this experience.

Julie enjoys gardening and bird watching in her backyard; she appreciates the beauty of nature.

Her love of nature and enthusiasm to teach young learners was Julie's motivation to write this story.

She hopes to share her love and respect for nature with readers of all ages.

Printed in the USA
CPSIA information can be obtained
at www.ICGtesting.com
LVHW060550221223

767112LV00051B/1325